DAY BY DAY WITH GOD

Prayer book for children

By: Francoise Darcy-Berube
  John Paul Berube

Art and design:
  Tiziana Tabbia-Plomteux

A Division of
William H. Sadlier Inc.
New York
Chicago
Los Angeles

Special consultants

Dr Thomas Francoeur
Rev. John Gurrieri
Rev. James Hawker

The content of this book reflects the goal of *Sharing the Light of Faith* (NCD).

Imprimatur
  † Bernard Hubert
    Bishop of Saint-Jean-sur-Richelieu, Que.
    February 16, 1982

Quotations from Scripture are adapted from the *Good News Bible.*
Copyright © American Bible Society, 1966, 1971, 1978.

Contents

A personal message 4
Why should we pray? 6
What is prayer? 10
To pray in the morning and the evening 13
- in the morning.. 14
- in the evening 16
From one feast day to another: the Liturgical Year 22
- The Advent Season.. 24
- Christmas 28
- The Lenten Season 30
- Holy Week 36
- Easter Sunday 44
- The Paschal Season 46
- The feast of Ascension... 47
- The feast of Pentecost... 48
- The feast of the Holy Trinity.................................. 49
To prepare for Sunday Eucharist....................................... 50
To prepare for the sacrament of Reconciliation 62
To pray to the Blessed Virgin... 66
Prayers for different occasions 70
- For my birthday 71
- For my parents' birthday or for Mothers' and Fathers' Day 71
- When school resumes 72
- For my friends.. 72
- For meal time 73
- For a feast day 73
- When I feel moody... 74
- When I am tempted to do wrong 74
- When I feel sad 74
- When someone I love is sick 75
- When I am sick.. 75
- When someone I love dies...................................... 76
- To profess my faith 77
- Praise to the Lord of the Universe............................. 78
- Prayer for our Planet Earth.................................... 79
- For the holidays 80

A personal message

We have written this prayer book for all children like you who want to be friends of Jesus. It may help you

- to understand better what prayer is about;
- to vary your daily prayers;
- to celebrate the great feasts of the Church Year;
- to prepare for Sunday Mass and also for the sacrament of Reconciliation;
- to pray to the Blessed Virgin;
- to discover how close God is to us each day.

For many years, we have tried to live as friends of Jesus. We have found it difficult at times, but we have gradually learned that it is a journey of joy. We wish to share that joy with you through this book. We hope you will enjoy praying with it as much as we enjoyed writing it for you!

Greetings from
Francoise and John Paul

**"The grace of the Lord Jesus Christ,
the love of God,
and the fellowship of the Holy Spirit
be with you all!"**

2 Corinthians 13: 13

Why should we pray?

Through the sacrament of Baptism, we become part of the Church, the Christian community which is God's family. We become children of God our Father who calls us to walk in the footsteps of Jesus. We receive the Spirit of God who will be with us always and teach us how to pray.

"If you will, come, follow me."

When you were baptized
your parents answered God's call
for you. Today, you are growing up,
and God is asking you to answer
the call for yourself.
He invites you to follow Him and
to live as a "child of light."

If you wish to answer God's call
and every day become a closer friend
of Jesus, you should pray often
in your heart. Then, as Jesus
promised, He will lead you along the
paths to eternal life.
Remember His words:

*"I am the light of the world. Whoever
follows Me will have the light of life
and will never walk in darkness."*

John 8: 12

Praise the Lord all people of the earth!
All you people of the earth sing for the Lord!

All around the world, at every moment,
people are praying, people are speaking to God
with words of love or praise,
of trust or thanksgiving.
It might be a whisper or a song...
But it always reaches to God's heart.

Prayer is so important that
some people have devoted
their whole life to it.
These people are like
the heart of the Church.

Many times during the day
and also through the night,
they gather to praise the Lord
in our name and in the name
of all those who do not know God.

They pray to God for all of us.
They pray for you, and me, too,
and everyone.
They pray that we may all live
as God's children,
that together we may build
a better world, a world of justice
and friendship for all.

How wonderful to know
that we are never alone
when we pray! The Church
is praying with us
all around the world!

What is prayer?

**Praying is thinking of God with love,
it is speaking to God in our heart.**

We can pray whenever we wish,
        wherever we wish,
        and however we wish.

God is always with us,
God always listens to us
because He loves us.
Nothing can separate us from God.

Often, throughout the day,
without anybody knowing,
we may speak to God in our heart
for a brief moment...

Nobody need ever know what we say
to the Lord; it is like a secret
between the two of us.
God is pleased when we speak to Him
and He gives us His peace.

Praying is also listening to God's Word and thinking about it in our heart.

When we like someone very much, we want to know our friend better. Jesus is our great friend. One way of getting to know Him better is to read the Gospel and think about it.

This is a way to think about the Gospel: slowly read a few lines and then pause for a moment and reflect. Ask the Holy Spirit to help you understand what God is saying to you through His Word.

For his First Communion, Kevin received a beautiful book of the Gospels. Sometimes he enjoys sitting quietly outside under a tree or in his room to read a Gospel story.

At Sheila's house, sometimes the whole family gets together to read the Gospel and talk about it. Each one shares his or her ideas to help one another to understand God's Word better.

Our bodies can help us to pray;
we can kneel, stand, sit or lie down.
What is important is that we are
comfortable and pray with respect.

Sometimes a gesture can help us
better say what we really mean.
During Mass, the priest often prays
with his arms outstretched or he may
bow in God's presence.

Like the children in the pictures,
we can pray with different gestures:

- to offer God our love with the new
  day,
- to give Him thanks and praise,
- to adore God or to say we are
  sorry for doing wrong.

To pray in the morning and the evening

Sing for the Lord
morning and evening!

Sing for the Lord
and bless His name!

"I will praise You, Lord,
with all my hearth;
I will tell of all
the wonderful things
You have done.
I will sing with joy
because of You.
I will sing praise to You,
almighty God!"

Psalms 9: 1-2

A new day is given to you; sing with joy to the Lord!

In the morning when you get up, you might still be sleepy, and have to hurry to get dressed, eat breakfast and get ready for school. You do not have time for a long prayer. But you can find some time while you are dressing, riding the bus or walking to school, to make the Sign of the Cross or to speak to God in your heart. God our Father gives us this bright new day; how could we begin it without saying: *"Thanks, I love You for it!"*

You might choose each morning one of the following prayers. To remind you to do so, you could leave your book open at this page, near your bed at night.

- To express your **love**

  † **My heart sings for You, o God,
  with the rising sun!
  I offer You my joy
  and praise You for this day!**

  † **God our Father,
  every one of my days
  is a gift of Your love.
  Help me love You in return.**

  † **To You, Lord, I offer
  the beauty of this earth.
  To You, Lord, I offer
  all of this day's work.
  To You, Lord, I offer
  my joy of being alive.**

- To express your **faith**

† **God our Father,**
  You create the world,
  You give us life,
  You share with us Your power,
  You adopt us as Your children.

  I believe in You.

† **Lord Jesus Christ,**
  beloved Son of the Father,
  You came to dwell among us.
  Through Your death
  and Resurrection,
  You give us eternal life.
  You remain with us
  through Your Spirit.

  I believe in You.

† **Holy Spirit,**
  Spirit of Jesus
  and of the Father,
  You live in our hearts
  and make us God's children.
  You enable us to love
  and be one family
  in the Church.

  I believe in You.

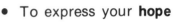

- To express your **hope**

† **God our Father,**
  You give me a heart
  so I can love and make people
  happy around me.
  Please help me do just that
  today and every day.
  I place my trust in You.

† **Lord Jesus,**
  You are my true friend.
  Today I have something
  really difficult to do...
  Please give me the courage
  to do it;
  knowing You are close to me
  will help me.

† **Holy Spirit,**
  help me during this day
  to love as Jesus did,
  so I can please the Father
  and truly be His child.

Night is falling, the day has gone... praise the Lord!

There are so many things we enjoy
doing in the evening...
We love to play, to read, to chat,
or to watch television for as long
as possible!

However, if you truly want to be
Jesus' friend, you will find time
to pray for a few minutes.

How do we pray in the evening?

It all depends:
just as our days are different,
so too the way we pray is different.
If we had a happy day, we might feel
like singing for God.
But if we had a difficult day,
we might prefer to share our troubles
with the Lord.
Some evenings we might like
to read a page in the Bible.

However, usually we do three
important things in our evening
prayer:
- we praise the Lord and give
  thanks;
- we think of our day
  and ask forgiveness for our sins;
- we pray with trust for ourselves,
  for those we love and
  for all the people of the earth,
  especially those who are lonely
  or suffering.

On the following pages you will find many different prayers. They will help you make up your very own manner of praying each evening:

- if you wish to give thanks,
  go to page 18;

- if you wish to ask for forgiveness,
  go to page 19;

- if you wish to express your trust
  in God and ask for help,
  go to pages 20 and 21.

Two prayers are very special to all of us and we like to say them often in the evening. You, too, can say them whenever you wish:

† **Our Father, who art in heaven,**
  hallowed be Thy name;
  Thy kingdom come;
  Thy will be done on earth
  as it is in heaven.
  Give us this day our daily bread;
  and forgive us our trespasses
  as we forgive those
  who trespass against us;
  and lead us not into temptation,
  but deliver us from evil. Amen.

† **Hail, Mary, full of grace,**
  the Lord is with you,
  blessed are you among women,
  and blessed is the fruit
  of your womb, Jesus.
  Holy Mary, Mother of God,
  pray for us, sinners,
  now and at the hour of our death.
  Amen.

Prayers to give thanks

- Think about your day
  and remember
  all the beautiful things
  you enjoyed,
  all that made you happy,
  all the good things you did.
  Tell God about them
  and thank Him.

- You might wish to use
  one of the following prayers:

† O Lord, God almighty,
  You do wonderful things for me:
  I can think and play,
  I can dream
  and make my dreams come true,
  I can make my own decisions
  and I can decide to love
  and make people happy.
  I thank You
  for the joy of being alive!

† God our Father,
  this day and every day
  it is You who gives me life.
  I thank You
  for Your great love;
  I want to love You
  with all my heart.

† Lord Jesus, my friend,
  today I had
  difficult things to do.
  You stood by me all along
  and helped me accomplish them.
  I love You and I thank You.

† Holy Spirit of God,
  this was a wonderful day,
  it was full of love and joy!
  All love comes from You;
  I thank You with all my heart.

Prayers to ask for forgiveness

- Remember: you are called to grow by developing your talents; you are called to love all the people around you.

- Think about your day:
  - Did you do on purpose something you knew would displease God?
  - Did you deliberately refuse to do something you knew God was asking you to do?

  If you did, tell Jesus about it. Say you are sorry and ask Him to help you do better tomorrow.

- You might wish to use one of the following prayers:

† **O my God, You are so good to me and I have offended You. Please forgive me and help me walk again on the paths of love.**

† **Lord God, have mercy on me for I have sinned. Because of Your great love, forgive me and heal me. And my heart shall be new and filled with Your joy!** From Psalms 51

"If you become angry, do not let your anger last into the night."

From Ephesians 4: 26

We all get angry sometimes, but the Lord asks us not to go to sleep angry.

If one evening you feel your heart is full of anger, the following prayer might help you overcome it and find peace:

† **Lord Jesus, I am still angry because... You know it is difficult for me to overcome my anger. Please help me do it and give me the courage to forgive and make peace with... as You want me to.**

Then decide what you will do tomorrow to make peace.

Prayers to express your trust and ask for help

Remember God's words:

"I love you with deep love,
My love for you shall never end."

Isaiah 54: 8-10

Remember also how kindly Jesus
welcomed all who came to Him,
children, the poor, the sick
and sinners.
He cared for each one of them,
He listened and did His best
to help them all.
In doing so, He showed us
how deeply God our Father
cares for us and loves us.

Remember Jesus' words:

"I will be with you always
to the end of time."

Matthew 28: 20

And Paul reminds us:

"Don't worry about anything,
but in all your prayers
ask God for what you need,
always asking Him
with a thankful heart.
And God's peace will be given
to you."

From Philippians 4: 6-7

We all have dreams and plans...
We also have our fears,
our worries, and our sorrows...
It is good to share all these
with God. He always listens to us
and understands us.
He wants to give us strength
and confidence so we will be able
to overcome our fears or
difficulties and make our dreams
come true.

Before going to sleep,
share your thoughts with the Lord
and ask for His help:

† **Lord Jesus, my friend,**
  You are always with me;
  I trust in You.
  Please help me, because...

It is good to pray also
for the people we love
and those who are in need of help
around the world.
You might use one of the following
prayers:

† **God our Father,**
I pray to You for all those
I love (name them).
Please bless them, protect them
and help them love You
more and more.

† **God our Father,**
You want our planet Earth
to be a happy home
for the entire human family.
But You know,
it is not like that right now.

> **Please, God, help us together**
> **make a better world for all.**

We pray for all those who are
suffering: the sick, the poor,
the hungry, the persecuted.

> **Please, God, help us together**
> **make a better world for all.**

We pray for those who have
no work, no friends, no home,
for the victims of violence
and for all those
in need of our prayer.

> **Please, God, help us together**
> **make a better world for all.**

Amen.

According to what is happening in the world today,
you might change or add to this prayer as you wish.

From one feast day to another...

All year round,
the Church invites us
to remember
the main events
in Jesus' life and
to celebrate them together.
This is what we call
the **Liturgical Year.**
It is like a festive road
which we walk together
every year,
joyously celebrating
the story of God's love
for us.

The Advent Season

The Liturgical Year begins with Advent. During Advent, we prepare our hearts for the Christmas celebration. It is exciting to feel Christmas is approaching!
We think of the presents, the tree, the parties... and we secretly prepare surprises!

But, by the way, why are you going to receive presents at Christmas?
It is not your birthday...
No, but it is Jesus' birthday!
Jesus is the most wonderful present God our Father has given to all and each one of us. It is in His honor that we give each other presents at Christmas.

The Christians in Germany have two beautiful customs for preparing for Christmas: the Advent wreath and the "Kristkindl." You might enjoy experiencing them with your family.

The "Kristkindl"

Since Christmas is Jesus' birthday, why not give Him a present? The best present we can offer Jesus is to put a little more love and happiness around us. This is what the "Kristkindl" is about; the word means Child-Jesus.

During the first week of Advent, each member of the family writes his or her name on a slip of paper. These are shuffled. Each person then draws a slip, and the name on it is his or her "Kristkindl." Every day a kind word or gesture will be said or done for one's "Kristkindl."

No one must know who is his or her "secret friend" but will probably guess it some day! And all the love and happiness in the family will be a wonderful birthday present for Jesus!

The Advent wreath

Four candles are fixed on a wreath made from fir or pine branches. The wreath represents the thousands of years during which the world awaited the coming of Jesus, and also the years since then that we have been waiting for the second coming of Jesus in glory.

Each week the family gathers to light a new candle and to sing and pray together in preparation for Christmas.

To help you pray during Advent

1st WEEK

Remember God's words:

*"God loved the world so much
that He gave His only Son so that
everyone who believes in Him
may have eternal life."*

From John 3: 16-17

Pray to the Lord:

† **God our Father,
because You love us so,
You gave us Your only Son
to free us from our sins
and guide us towards You.
We give You thanks and praise,
and we put all our trust in You.
Amen.**

2nd WEEK

Remember God's words:

*"You will be My friends
if you love one another."*

From John 15: 14-17

Pray to the Lord:

† **Lord Jesus,
You want everyone to be happy
to celebrate Your birth,
but many people around us
are sad and lonely.
Help us reach out to them
and comfort them with our love,
so they, too, can celebrate
Christmas with hope and joy.
Amen.**

Remember God's words:

"I say it again, rejoice!
The Lord is coming soon.
Be gentle toward everyone.
And the peace of God
will be with you."

From Philippians 4: 4-8

Pray to the Lord:

† **God our Father,**
Christmas is coming, I can't wait!
Open my heart to Your word
so I can prepare with great love
for the coming of Jesus. Amen.

Remember God's words:

"I am the light of the world.
Whoever follows Me will have
the light of life and will never
walk in darkness."

John 8: 12

Pray to the Lord:

† **Lord Jesus,**
You are the light of the world
and I believe in You.
I want to walk in Your footsteps
so You can guide me to the Father
on the paths of eternal life.
Amen.

Christmas is here!

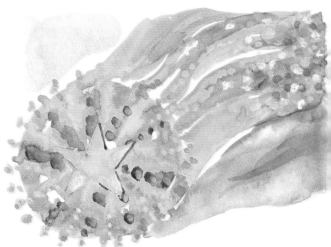

"The angel said to the sheperds:
I am here with a good news for you,
which will bring great joy
to all the people. This very day,
your Saviour was born,
Christ the Lord!"

Luke 2: 10-12

"Glory to God in the highest
heaven, and peace on earth
to all people whom God loves!"

Luke 2: 14

To help you pray during the Christmas Season

Prayer to God our Father

† **God our Father,**
we give You thanks and praise
for the great love
You have bestowed upon us
in giving us Your Son Jesus.
With love we offer You in return
the happy days we are celebrating
in honor of Jesus. Amen.

Prayer to the Lord Jesus

† **Lord Jesus,**
You are the most wonderful present
God our Father ever gave
to all the people of the earth!
With them I thank You
and I love You for coming
to dwell among us. Amen.

Prayer to the Blessed Virgin

† **Holy Mary,**
I think of your joy when you saw
your baby Jesus for the first time!
Today it is my turn to rejoice
because I know Jesus
and He is my friend!
Help me love Him
and follow Him faithfully,
as you did all your life. Amen.

The Lenten Season

During Lent, with the whole Christian community we fervently prepare for the greatest feast of the year: Easter.

A family activity for Lent

Make up your own Lenten activity, for instance: bring in a branch that is beginning to bud, put it in water and watch the flowers open. Or plant seeds in a carton, then watch them die and come to life. Or, if you wish, experience with your family what Nick and Joyce did with their family.

In their part of the country the ground is still covered with snow during Lent, and there are no leaves or flowers on the trees. So, one day, they brought home branches of dead wood. Using color tissue paper cut in small circles and tied up with thread, they prepared a box of little paper flowers.

Each Saturday Nick, Joyce and their parents took a few minutes to prepare for Sunday Mass. They hung a few flowers on the branches while offering to God their work and efforts of the past week. Then they said the following prayer:

† **Lord Jesus,**
to prepare ourselves for the
great feast of Your Resurrection,
we have tried during this week
to do our work better and to care
for one another even more.
We now offer You our efforts
with our love.
May we arrive at Easter
with a renewed and happy heart.
Amen.

On Easter morning, Nick and Joyce
placed the branches that had come
to life with paper flowers near
the crucifix. It was like a bouquet
of love and joy that they offered
to the Risen Christ. Then they lit
a candle, and together the family
sang an Easter song.

**"Let the Spirit
direct your lives...
Let love make you
serve one another...**

From Galatians 5

A time for sharing

During Lent, the Christian community, in the name of the Lord, invites us to share what we have with those who have less.

There are in the world millions of people who go hungry every day. There are children who have no home, no school, no medical care. This is a way your family could help them:

Make a money-box and ask each person in your family to put in a little money every time they are willing to go without something extra, like a candy bar, a pack of cigarettes, a little toy, a magazine, etc. — Maybe neighboring families might like to take part in the project. — At the end of Lent, give the money to an organization that takes care of refugees or other needy people at home or abroad.

If you prefer, you could gather food, clothes, and toys instead of money.

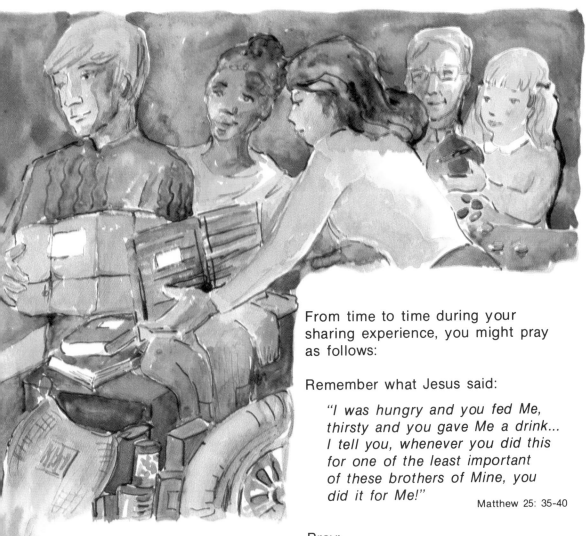

"God loves the one who gives gladly."

2 Corinthians 9: 7

Whatever we do for one another,
we truly do for Jesus Himself.
But, if we are not willing
to care and to share, we cannot
be Jesus' friends.

From time to time during your
sharing experience, you might pray
as follows:

Remember what Jesus said:

*"I was hungry and you fed Me,
thirsty and you gave Me a drink...
I tell you, whenever you did this
for one of the least important
of these brothers of Mine, you
did it for Me!"*

Matthew 25: 35-40

Pray:

† **God our Father,
You gave us this earth as our home,
and You want its resources to be used
for the good of all Your children.
Teach us to share whatever we have
with those who do not have as much.
We ask this through Christ our Lord.
Amen.**

A time for conversion and renewal

Lent is a time to be converted. What is conversion? The story of Zacchaeus can help us answer this question.

Zacchaeus was a tax collector. People disliked him because he was a cheat. He often put in his own pocket money he was receiving as taxes.

One day, Jesus came to Zacchaeus's town, but Zacchaeus was very small and he could not see Jesus because of the crowd. He then climbed up into a tree so that he could see.

When Jesus came close to the tree, He looked up and said: *"Hurry down, Zacchaeus. I want to come to your house today."* Zacchaeus hurried down and welcomed Him with great joy.

This is when Zacchaeus was converted, when he changed his heart. In listening to Jesus talk about the Kingdom of God, he understood what he had done wrong and what God was asking of him. He said to Jesus: *"Listen, Lord, I will give half my money to the poor, and to those I have cheated I will pay back four times as much."* Jesus smiled at Zacchaeus and said: *"Today you have been saved. For I have come to save people who are lost."* From Luke 19: 1-11

During Lent God calls us to change our hearts, to acknowledge our faults and decide how we want to grow in love. If you wish to answer that call, you might set aside a quiet time one evening and use this page to reflect and pray.

1. Listen to God's words:

   "Come back to the Lord your God. He is kind and full of mercy." Joel 2: 12

   "I will give you a new heart and a new mind, I will put My Spirit in you." Ezechiel 36: 26

2. Remember what God asks of you: that you love Him with all your heart:
   - praying to Him each day,
   - putting your trust in Him;

   that you love your neighbor:
   - respecting others and their belongings,
   - caring, sharing and being kind to others,
   - learning to forgive and be reconciled;

   that you love yourself:
   - taking care of yourself and respecting your body,
   - developing your talents and good qualities,
   - having self-confidence and not getting discouraged.

3. Think about what you have done wrong, especially if it occurs repeatedly.

4. Ask for forgiveness:

   † **O my God, please forgive me for I have sinned against You. I trust in Your love and with Your help I will try to do better. Amen.**

5. Decide what you want to do to better answer God's call. Your efforts will unite you to all other Christians around the world who are trying like you to truly live the Lenten Season.

6. Then pray the following prayer:

   † **God our Father, please help us improve and grow during this Lent. We would like to reach Easter with a new and more loving heart. We ask You this through Jesus Your Son. Amen.**

If you wish to celebrate the sacrament of Reconciliation during Lent, see pages 62 to 65.

Holy week

During Holy Week, which is the week before Easter, we remember and celebrate the last days that Jesus spent on this earth.

- **On Palm Sunday,** we recall the triumphant entry of Jesus into Jerusalem.

- **On Holy Thursday,** we commemorate in the Eucharist the Last Supper of Jesus with His friends.

- **On Good Friday,** we remember the death of Jesus on the cross.

- **On Easter morning,** we celebrate in jubilation the glorious Resurrection of Jesus.

Holy Week is such an important time for Christians around the world that each year thousands of people from many countries make a pilgrimage to the Holy Land so they can celebrate the Holy Days right there where Jesus died and rose for our salvation. The pilgrims make the Way of the Cross on the very road Jesus walked on His way to Calvary. Some of them carry a cross on their shoulders.

There are people who save their money for many years to make that pilgrimage. They do it to show their love for Jesus and their will to follow Him ever more closely.

To prepare for the different and beautiful celebrations of Holy Week, before going to church, you might read the pages that concern each day.

If you cannot go to church on a given day, you could find quiet time at home to read the page for that day and pray in your heart.

Palm Sunday

On this day, we recall the joyful celebration
that the people of Jerusalem
prepared for Jesus
a few days before He died.

Jesus had brought his friend Lazarus back
to life. Hearing about it, the people of
Jerusalem got excited and enthusiastic.
When they learned that Jesus was entering
the city, they hastily prepared a joyful
parade, laying their coats on the path,
waving palm branches and singing for Him:
*"Blessed is He Who comes in the name
of the Lord! Hosannah in the highest!"*

Today in church we, too, make a procession
in honor of Jesus. We sing the same song
and hold palms in our hands. We also bring
the palms home to remind us of Jesus all
year round.

Here is a prayer you could say at home when you bring back your palm:

† **Lord Jesus,**
  you are our King and our Saviour.
  It is to honor You that we have sung
  and carried these palms.
  Bless the houses where they will
  be placed.
  Deliver us from all evil
  and protect us through Your love.
  Amen.

During the Eucharist which follows the procession, we listen with respect to the story of Jesus' Passion. We will meditate all week on that story and we will learn to what extent Jesus has loved us and with what courage He gave His life for us.

Holy Thursday

On this day, we remember
and celebrate Jesus' Last Supper
with His friends.

On the evening before He died,
Jesus wanted to share with His
friends the Passover meal. During
that meal He did, for them and for
us, something wonderful:

*"He took a piece of bread, gave
thanks to God, broke it, and gave it
to them saying:
This is My body which is given for
you. Do this in memory of Me."*

Luke 22: 19

Today, every time we share the
Bread of Life during Mass, Jesus
truly gives Himself to us under the
sign of the bread. He comes to us so
we may be filled with love, courage
and trust, in our everyday life.

This is what you could do to prepare
for the Holy Thursday celebration:

Think about these words of Jesus:

*"I am the Living Bread that came
down from heaven.
If anyone eats this bread,
he will live for ever.
Whoever eats My body has eternal life,
and I will raise him to life
on the last day."*

From John 6: 51-58

Then pray this prayer:

† **Lord Jesus,
You work wonders for me.
You come to dwell in my heart
when I receive the Bread of Life.
I love You and I thank You.
Teach me how to please the Father
and become Your friend
more and more.
Praise to You, Lord Jesus Christ!**

Before going to church, think of the
special things you want to say to
Jesus today after communion.

If you are not able to go to church,
take a little time to pray and reflect
at home, using these pages.

Good Friday

On this very special day, we remember that Jesus gave His life for us.

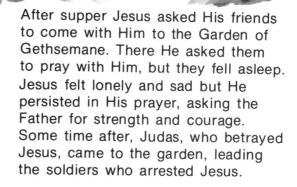

After supper Jesus asked His friends to come with Him to the Garden of Gethsemane. There He asked them to pray with Him, but they fell asleep. Jesus felt lonely and sad but He persisted in His prayer, asking the Father for strength and courage. Some time after, Judas, who betrayed Jesus, came to the garden, leading the soldiers who arrested Jesus.

All night long, the soldiers and others made fun of Jesus and tortured Him, while Jesus remained silent. Peter, during that time, turned his back on Jesus, denying he even knew Him. Finally, Jesus was sentenced to death. He carried His heavy cross to Mount Calvary. There He was nailed to the cross between two thieves.

Jesus was in terrible pain; still He found the courage to pray, asking His Father to forgive those who had crucified Him. Only one of His apostles, John, was there. Jesus asked John to take care of His mother Mary who was standing by the cross. Then He prayed again, crying out in a loud voice: *"Father, in Your hands I commend My spirit."* And He died.

In giving up His life for us with such great love, Jesus saved us from the power of evil and opened for us the paths of eternal life.

In church, on this day, we read again the story of the Passion. We honor the cross of Jesus by bowing in front of it or kissing it. We receive Holy Communion. We pray for all the people of the earth from whom Jesus gave His life. We can also make the Way of the Cross.

You can prepare yourself for the celebration by doing the following:

- Quietly look at the pictures on this page, remembering what you just read about the sufferings of Jesus. Then read these words:

"If anyone wants to come with Me, he must forget himself, take up his cross every day and follow Me." Luke 9: 23

To forget oneself and carry one's cross means:
- to work hard at developing and growing as a person;
- to accept sacrifices sometimes to help others and make them happy.

When we forget ourselves to take care of others, we are, in our own way, giving our life like Jesus.

- Speak to Jesus in your heart. Then pray as follows:

† **Lord Jesus,
You gave Your life to save us.
I love You and I thank You
for Your great love.**

† **Lord Jesus,
You forgave those who crucified You.
Please give me the courage
to forgive those who hurt me.**

† **Lord Jesus,
You ask us sometimes to forget ourselves
so we can better care for others
and make them happy.
Please help me grow in love
so I will do just that,
as You did for us. Amen.**

Easter Sunday

This is the happiest day of the year for Christians around the world!

*"Early on Sunday morning,
the women went to the tomb...
They found the stone
rolled away from the entrance
of the tomb, so they went in;
but they did not find
the body of the Lord Jesus.*

*They stood there puzzled,
when suddenly two men
in bright shining clothes
stood by them and said:*

*Why are you looking
among the dead
for One Who is alive?
He is not here,
He has been raised...
as He said He would.*

From Luke 24: 1-7

During the following days Jesus appeared to Peter, John, Mary of Magdala and to many others. All were stunned and full of wonder. They had been very depressed after Jesus died. But now their hearts were full of joy and they said to one another: *"Yes, it is true. The Lord is risen indeed!"*

From Luke 24: 34

**"This is the day
of the Lord's victory;
let us be happy,
let us celebrate!"**

Psalms 118: 24

In church, we commemorate the Resurrection of Jesus in a very unique and beautiful celebration which is held during the night. It is called the **Paschal Vigil.** During that night many things happen:

- We light the Paschal candle. Its flame is the symbol of the new life of the Risen Christ. Each person comes to light a small candle at that flame, for we all share in this new life.

- Then, together, we proclaim our faith.
  The priest asks us:
  "Do you believe in Jesus Christ, Who has been raised from the dead?"

  And the whole community answers with one heart:
  "Yes, we do believe."

- Oftentimes children or adults are baptized during the Vigil.

- Finally we celebrate in the Eucharist the death and Resurrection of Jesus.

To prepare yourself for this great celebration and also during the following days of Easter week you could say this prayer:

† **God our Father, through the Resurrection of Jesus You have filled the whole world with new hope and joy. Fill our own hearts with that Easter joy and help us share it with all those who have not yet heard the Good News. We ask this through Christ our Lord. Amen.**

The Paschal Season

During the fifty days of the Paschal Season we continue to live in the joy of Easter. The following prayers might help you during that special time.

Prayer to the Risen Lord

† **Praise and glory to You, Lord Jesus!**

**By the mystery of Your Resurrection
You fill my heart with a wonderful hope:
one day, like You, I will overcome death and
I will join You near the Father for ever and ever.**

Praise and glory to You, Lord Jesus!

**Like You did on Easter morn with Mary of Magdala,
You call me by my name. You bid me be Your friend,
and on the path of my life You are always with me.**

Praise and glory to You, Lord Jesus!

**In the new world where You live shines the glory
of our God. He is a God of light and bids us
live together as children of the light.**

Praise and glory to You, Lord Jesus!

Prayer to the Blessed Virgin

† **Queen of heaven, rejoice, alleluia!
The Son Whom it was your privilege
to bear, alleluia,
has risen as He said, alleluia!
Pray God for us, alleluia!**

**V. Rejoice and be glad, Virgin Mary, alleluia!
R. For the Lord has truly risen, alleluia!**

**O God, You were pleased to give joy to the world
through the Resurrection of Your Son,
our Lord Jesus Christ. Grant we beseech You,
that through the prayers of the Virgin Mary,
His mother, we may come to possess the joys
of life everlasting. Through Christ our Lord. Amen.**

The feast of Ascension

Forty days after Easter Jesus said good-bye to His friends. He bid them spread the Good News of His Resurrection to all the people of the world. Then He left this earth and went back to His Father from whence He will return at the end of time to transform in glory the whole universe.

We celebrate the Ascension of the Lord a few weeks after Easter.
To prepare for that feast you could do the following:

- Remember God's Word:

*"I am going to prepare a place for you in My Father's house.
And after I go and prepare a place for you, I will come back and take you to Myself, so that you will be where I am."*

John 14: 3-4

*"Give thanks to the Lord,
because He is good;
His love is eternal."*

Psalms 136: 1

- Pray to God our Father

† **God our Father,
You have made us Your children,
and You want to gather in Your house
all the people of the earth.
Send Your messengers
all around the world
so they can spread the Good News.
We ask You this
through Christ our Lord. Amen.**

- Pray to Jesus

† **Lord Jesus,
You are alive and You are with us.
You are our light and our guide.
Help us walk
on the path of eternal life
so we can be with You
for ever and ever. Amen.**

The feast of Pentecost

Before returning to the Father, Jesus had promised His friends He would send them the Holy Spirit. This He did on Pentecost day.

The Holy Spirit is given to us also in a very special way through the sacraments of Baptism and Confirmation.

You might use the following prayers to prepare for the feast of Pentecost or at any time during the year to pray to the Holy Spirit.

Prayer to God our Father

† **God our Father,**
You work wonders for us,
You give us Your Spirit
through the Sacraments.
May Your Spirit help us
to know and love You better,
and to care for one another.
We ask You this
through Christ our Lord. Amen.

Prayers to the Holy Spirit

† **Holy Spirit,**
You make us one
with Jesus and the Father.
You help us understand God's Word.
You teach us how to pray and
how to love one another.
You give us the peace and joy
of Jesus.
I love You and I thank You.
Glory to You, Holy Spirit of God,
now and for ever. Amen.

† **Come, Holy Spirit,**
fill our hearts with the warmth
of Your love.
Come, transform the hearts of all
the people of the earth,
so they can build together
a better world. Amen.

† **Come, Holy Spirit,**
help me see and do what is right.
Help me walk in Jesus' way of
happiness. Amen.

With the feast of Pentecost, the Paschal Season comes to a close. The following Sundays are part of the **Ordinary Time** of the Liturgical Year.

The feast of the Holy Trinity

We celebrate this feast on the Sunday following Pentecost. You can prepare for it by reading this page carefully.

Jesus often spoke to His friends of God His Father and also of the Spirit who was always with Him. In doing that, He revealed to us the wonderful and mysterious secret of God's own life. Thus we understand a little better who is our God:

God is the Father, the Son and the Holy Spirit. The Three are one in love. The Three are the Blessed Trinity.

This is why the most beautiful thing we can say about God is what John the apostle wrote: **"God is Love."** John wrote another important thing:

"Whoever does not love cannot be a friend of God... Whoever loves is a child of God and knows God. No one has ever seen God, but if we love one another, God lives in us."

From I John 4: 8-13

Whenever you want to adore and praise the **Blessed Trinity** you might choose one of the following prayers:

† **Glory be to the Father,**
and to the Son,
and to the Holy Spirit.
As it was in the beginning,
is now, and ever shall be
world without end. Amen.

† **We give thanks and praise to You,**
God almighty,
Father, Son and Holy Spirit,
now and for ever. Amen. Alleluia!

† **We worship You,**
we adore You,
we praise You,
O Blessed Trinity.
We sing to the glory of Your name.
Amen. Alleluia!

To prepare for all other Sundays, you will find help on pages 50 to 62.

To prepare for Sunday Eucharist

"Come,
let us sing with joy for the Lord!"

Psalms 95

**It is a privilege to be invited,
it makes us feel proud and happy!**

Have you ever thought about
this: the Lord Himself is inviting
you to meet Him in the
Eucharist! Your parish community
also invites you to come and
share the Bread of Life. Who
could forget or refuse such an
invitation? If you were not there,
someone, for sure, would be
missing from the celebration!

This is the day of the Lord, this is a day of joy!

Our brothers and sisters, the first Christians called Sunday the **Lord's day,** which means the day of the Risen Jesus. For them, each Sunday was like another Easter day, and no one could be sad on such a day! All were invited to relax, to rejoice and, of course, to gather for the Eucharist.

For us also Sunday is special. It begins in the morning: we can sleep longer, take our time for breakfast, and we sometimes put on different clothes... During the day we often visit or welcome friends and have a good time, playing or going out for our favorite sport; we have special programs on TV; sometimes a surprise dessert awaits us at the family meal!

And, of course, there is Mass! This is what is most special about our Sunday. That weekly encounter with Jesus in our parish community is so important that we should prepare for it carefully. Remember the story of the *Little Prince* and his friend the fox, how the fox explained that before meeting a great friend we ought to "dress up our heart"!

If you want to "dress up your heart" for your encounter with Jesus, you will find the help you need in pages 50 to 62. On Saturday evening or before Mass, each week choose one or two of these pages and take a few minutes to read them carefully. You will then be ready to enjoy and share more fully in the Sunday Eucharist with your parish community.

"When two or three come together in My name, I am there with them."

Matthew 18: 20

Preparing to listen to God's Word

What are we doing on this earth?
How can we find the path to true happiness
and fullness of life? Those questions are difficult.
No one can find the answers without God's help.

Fortunately, God has spoken to us in many
different ways, and, most of all, through
His Son Jesus. To each one of us God, talking
about Jesus, says: *"This is My own dear Son,
listen to Him."*
Mark 9: 7

Jesus Himself tells us He came to guide us
on the path of true life: *"I have come in order
that you might have life, life in all its
fullness."*
John 10: 10

Speaking of His Resurrection which brings eternal
life to all humankind, Jesus also said: *"I will see
you again, and your hearts will be filled with
gladness, the kind of gladness that no one can
take away from you."*
John 16: 22

The words of God are words of life and hope;
they are the light of our path; that is why every
time we celebrate the Eucharist we share God's
Word and try to understand it better.

But listening to God's Word also means putting it into practice. When we really trust someone, we know that what this person asks of us is truly for our own good.

See for example what Nick and Caroline did. They had just become members of a folk dance club. They were enthusiastic, and their teacher told them they were very gifted, and could even enter the next regional contest if they worked very hard and spent most of their leisure time rehearsing. Because they trusted their teacher, they accepted her word, they sacrificed many other activities and they achieved their dream.

Next time you go to Mass, try to listen closely to the readings and homily; through them God is truly speaking to you. To prepare your heart, you might say the following prayer right now:

† **Lord Jesus,**
 I firmly believe You want to lead me
 on the path of happiness
 and fullness of life.
 I trust You, and want
 to follow You closely.
 Please give me Your Spirit
 so I can better understand Your Word
 and be faithful to it in my daily life.
 Amen.

"You spoke to me, and I listened to every word. Your words filled my heart with joy and happiness!" Jeremiah 15: 16

Preparing to give thanks to God

Are you ever filled with such wonder and joy that you feel like singing or dancing to express your gratitude? Like when someone surprises you with a wonderful gift, or when, after a long separation, you are reunited with someone you love very much?

Now consider this: if we really understood who is our God, how much He loves us and does for us, wouldn't we be filled with wonder and feel like singing for joy?

That is why the priest at Mass, like the Bible often does, invites us to praise God and give Him thanks with all our heart. Listen to the psalmist:

"Come, and see what God has done!
Say to God, how wonderful are the things You do!
Praise God with shouts of joy, all peoples!
Sing to the glory of His name."   From Psalms 66 and 136

To prepare for giving thanks at Mass, you might do the following:

- Think of all that made you happy this week:
    beautiful things you saw,
    your successes in work or sport, etc.,
    the people and activities you enjoyed,
    the good things you did...

  You will carry all that in your heart when you join your community in giving thanks during Mass.

- Now read the following prayer slowly.

Prayer to give thanks

† I praise You, my God, for Your love is eternal!
I give You thanks with all my heart.

Lord God, Father almighty, You created the universe
and all creatures that dwell in it.
You made us in Your likeness.
You share with us Your power.
You entrust the world to our care,
and invite us to enjoy it.

I praise You, my God, for Your love is eternal!
I give You thanks with all my heart.

Jesus Your Son came to us to reveal to us Your love.
He welcomed the children and cured the sick.
He freed us from sin and taught us Your ways.
He gave us Your Spirit to be with us always.

I praise You, my God, for Your love is eternal!
I give You thanks with all my heart.

Preparing to offer our life with Jesus

Every time we share in the Eucharist, we remember that Jesus gave His life to save us. We also celebrate His Resurrection and the wonderful promise He made that He would return at the end of time to raise us and take us with Him. That is why at Mass we joyfully say or sing together:

**"Christ has died,
Christ is risen,
Christ will come again."**

In giving His life for us, Jesus set an example. If we truly want to be His friends, we, too, should give our life by loving and serving one another. This is what we mean when we present to God the bread and the wine that will become the Body and Blood of Christ. God our Father then welcomes our offering with that of Jesus.

To prepare for offering your life with Jesus you might do the following:

- Think about what you did during the week: your schoolwork, your efforts to help at home, to care for and share with your family and friends...

  Think also about your worries, your problems, what might frighten or sadden you...

  Think about your dreams and plans, about what you would like to achieve in the coming week...

- Then say the following prayer:

† **God our Father,**
tomorrow at Mass the priest will offer You
the bread and wine.
With him, I offer You each day of my life,
my work and my dreams,
my love and my pains.
As the bread and wine will be changed
into the Body and Blood of Jesus,
may my heart and my life be transformed
and filled with Your love.
I ask this through Christ our Lord.
Amen.

"The greatest love
a person can have for his friends
is to give his life for them."

John 15: 13

Preparing to share in the Bread of Life

Inviting someone to share a meal is like saying to that person:

"We wish to get closer to you; come, we will share our thoughts and our dreams while sharing our bread. That will help us know each other better and become closer to one another."

Being invited to share in the Eucharist means somewhat the same thing. That is why the priest says to us before Communion:

"Happy are those who are called to the Lord's supper!"

Isn't it wonderful to be God's own guests! To live this very special meeting with Jesus to the full, here is what you could do:

• **Before going to Mass**

- Remember what Jesus said:

"I am the Living Bread that came down from heaven. If anyone eats this Bread, he lives in Me, and I live in him. If anyone eats this Bread, he will live for ever, and I will raise him to life on the last day."
From John 6: 51-58

"You are My friends, if you do what I command you. This is what I command you: love one another."
John 15: 14-17

- Think about it:

To thrive and grow, we share daily the bread of the earth. To thrive and grow as children of God we need the bread that comes from heaven, we need Jesus and His Spirit. That is why we receive Holy Communion as often as we can.

- Pray to Jesus:

† **Lord Jesus, just as Zacchaeus gladly welcomed You in his house so, too, I welcome You gladly in my heart. Teach me to walk closely with You on the paths of love. Amen.**

- **At Mass, after Communion**

Take advantage of the few minutes after Communion to speak in your heart to Jesus. He comes to make you closer to Him and help you live as a "child of light." Pray as you wish.

The following prayers may also help you at that time:

† **Lord Jesus, You come to me to give me God's own life. I adore You and I thank You.**

† **Lord Jesus, You are my friend and my guide, I love You and I trust You. Help me be faithful to You.**

† **Lord Jesus, please give me Your Spirit, so I can truly love as You did and thus please the Father.**

- **When you leave church**

Mass is ended but life goes on, and the priest sends us forth: *"Go in peace, to love and serve the Lord."* As the song goes: *"And they'll know we are Christians, by our love!"*

Now remember, Jesus is with you at all times. Have a wonderful week, full of love, friendship and joy!

To prepare for the sacrament of Reconciliation

We know how God is calling us to live and act. Saint Paul says it beautifully: *"Try to be like God, since you are His dear children. Follow a path of love as Jesus did."*
Ephesians 5: 1

Often we answer God's call. But, sometimes, we do not. Sometimes we choose to do wrong; we sin. This happens to all of us; we are all sinners.

However, God is always willing to forgive us if we turn back to Him. This is why the Church invites us to celebrate the loving forgiveness of God in the sacrament of Reconciliation.

Sometimes we celebrate the sacrament with other Christians. Other times, we prefer to go to the priest alone and celebrate it with him. Whichever way we prefer, it is always the Lord and the community who welcome us through the priest.

How to prepare before confession

- **Pray to the Holy Spirit:**

† **Holy Spirit, please help me
to understand God's call,
to know my sins
and regret them with all my heart.**

- **Think about your life:**

    The following questions might help you:

    - Do I neglect to pray to the Lord each day?

    - Do I sometimes close my heart to others,
      refusing to understand them, to help them
      or share with them?

    - When I get angry, do I refuse to be
      reconciled?

    - Do I harm others
        by stealing or speaking ill of them?
        by making fun of them?
        by hurting them, specially younger
            ones?
        by leading them to do wrong?

    - Does it happen
        that I take revenge?
        that I lie or cheat?
        that I show disrespect for my body
            or that of others?

- **Ask God for His forgiveness:**

† **O my God, I am sorry for my sins.
In choosing to sin and failing to do good,
I have sinned against You and Your Church.
I firmly intend, with the help of Your Son,
to make up for my sins, and to live as I should.**

Celebrating the individual rite of Reconciliation

- The priest welcomes you in the name of Jesus and of the Church. Together you make the Sign of the Cross.

  The priest talks with you and may read to you from the Bible.

- As if you were speaking to Jesus, you tell the priest about your sins and why you think you acted that way.

  The priest talks to you to help you regret your sins and to encourage you to do better.

  He gives you a penance to make up for your sins.

  You then pray the Act of Contrition.

- The priest gives you absolution by saying:

  **"I forgive you your sins
  in the name of the Father,
  and of the Son,
  and of the Holy Spirit."**

  You answer: **"Amen."**

  The priest says:

  **"Give thanks to the Lord,
  for He is good!"**

  You answer:

  "His mercy endures for ever."

  You say good-bye to the priest and thank him.

What to do after confession

- Give thanks to God for having forgiven you,
  and ask His help for doing better.

- Decide what special effort you want to make so you will grow in love
  and better answer God's call.

- Think about doing the penance the priest gave you.

"When we love one another, we live in the light." From I John 2: 10

† **O Lord, You do wonderful things for me:**
You forgive all my sins,
You make me able to love,
You give me Your own peace and Your joy.
I give You thanks with all my heart.

To pray to the Blessed Virgin

The Virgin Mary holds a special place in our heart for she is Jesus' mother. We often think of her and pray to her, especially during the months of May and October, and on her feastdays.

To honor and pray to Mary, we say the Rosary while we remember some important events in the lives of Jesus and Mary. These events we call the **Mysteries of the Rosary.**

If you would like to say the Rosary as many of us do around the world, you can use the following pages.

The Joyful Mysteries

When she was living on earth,
Mary shared with Joseph
many wonderful events.
One of her greatest joys
was of course
to gaze for the first time
on her tiny baby Jesus!
These happy events we call
the **Joyful Mysteries.**

Today, we, too,
can rejoice with Mary,
for the coming of Jesus
is good news
which fills the world
with hope:
- Jesus comes to us,
- He is our friend and brother,
- He leads us to the Father.

If you want to share in
Mary's Joyful Mysteries, this
is what you can do: slowly
say the **Hail Mary** and think
of Jesus' mother, picture her
- when she was expecting
  Jesus,
- when she lay Him in
  the crib,
- when she took care of
  Him,
- when she watched Him
  grow and work with
  Joseph.

You may say the **Hail Mary**
as many times as you want
in thinking of these Joyful
Mysteries.

The Sorrowful Mysteries

Near the cross, Mary is crying.
Something terrible has happened to Jesus,
he was arrested by His enemies
and sentenced to death.

Mary remembers all the wonderful
things He did for His people and she
can't believe what they have done
to Him!

But she can do nothing.
So she stands by her Son,
sharing His pain and agony.
She loves Him, and prays in silence.

If you love Mary, think of her pain
and sorrow during those terrible days.
While slowly saying the **Hail Mary**,
remember these **Sorrowful Mysteries**
in the lives of Jesus and Mary:

- Mary learns that Jesus has been
  sentenced to death;

- she sees Him carrying His heavy
  cross;

- she hears the crowd insulting Him;

- she stands by Him when He is
  crucified;

- she sees Him die on the cross.

You may say the **Hail Mary** as many
times as you want in thinking of
these Sorrowful Mysteries.

The Glorious Mysteries

After Good Friday came **Easter,** the unforgettable day when Jesus rose from the dead!

That wonderful event filled Mary's heart with incredible happiness: her beloved Son had overcome death, He had entered a new life that would last forever.
It was God's own eternal life.
This, indeed, was a **Glorious Mystery!**

There were other great events like the **Ascension** when Jesus returned to the Father, and **Pentecost** when Mary and Jesus' friends were filled with the Spirit. Later on, when the time came for Mary to return to the Father, Jesus came to get her and she shared fully in His Resurrection. This we call the mystery of the **Assumption.**

Think of these Glorious Mysteries while slowly praying the **Hail Mary**. Remember Jesus and Mary are with the Father; they love you and want to help you join them when the time comes for you.

You may say the **Hail Mary** as many times as you want in thinking of these Glorious Mysteries.

Prayers for different occasions

As the seasons of the year, our life changes... This last part of your book contains many prayers for different occasions. Of course, you will not find a prayer for every single event in your life... Just imagine the number of pages we would need for that!

But there is one thing you can do to suit your needs: on a special occasion, or when you feel like it, make up your own prayer and write it on a sheet of paper the size of this book. Then place it in the book wherever you wish. You might also like to illustrate it with a drawing. Doing that will enrich your prayer book, making it even more your own, and will enable you to say those prayers again whenever you want.

For my birthday

✝ **Lord Jesus,**
today is my birthday!
I am now... years old!
I had a cake with... candles.
I received many gifts and
everyone was so nice to me.
I wish it were my birthday
every day!
Thank You, Lord,
for all that happiness.

You know, Jesus, I am happy
to be growing up:
I can do more things,
stay up later,
enjoy more freedom,
and I like that.

But sometimes I find it difficult
to be growing up:
people make more demands on me,
they expect me to be more reasonable
and responsible... and sometimes
I just don't feel like it!

Nevertheless, it is good to grow up!
Help me be proud of it
and happy to take on
more responsibilities.

I pray, Lord Jesus, for all those
who care for me
and made this day wonderful.
Help me love them even more
in return. Amen.

For my parents' birthday or for Mothers' and Fathers' Day

On these special occasions why not write your own prayer? Nobody knows but you what you truly want to say to God about your parents!

Think of all they mean to you; write your prayer on a nice sheet of paper, illustrate it and pray it.
Then you might want to give it to them. And next year, you can make up another one.

When school resumes

† Lord Jesus,
vacation is over
and I feel a bit sad.
But I have wonderful memories
to enjoy and I thank You for that.

Tomorrow school begins:
I'll have to get working again!
As You know, Lord,
some things I enjoy in school,
others I don't...
Please help me work hard anyway,
so I can develop my talents
as You want me to.
I will then be able one day
to achieve what I want,
to make my dreams come true,
and be of service to others.
Amen.

For my friends

† Lord Jesus,
it's wonderful to have friends:
we can have so much fun together!
You know that for You, too,
had Your friends.

But friendship is not always easy:
our friends have shortcomings,
and so do we!
Sometimes we quarrel and fight;
we might even get so angry
that we feel like breaking up...

Please, Jesus, help me be patient
and generous with my friends,
help me understand
and encourage them.
Help me to make up promptly
after a dispute.

Lord Jesus,
I pray for all my friends;
bless them and help us grow up
happily together. Amen.

For meal time

† **God our Father,
as we gladly share our food,
may we also share ourselves and
grow together in Your love. Amen.**

† **Lord God, we give You thanks for
this meal which will renew our strength.
Bless those who prepared it and keep us
all united in Your love. Amen.**

† **Lord, God of all creation,
bless this food
which is the fruit of the earth
and of the work of human hands.
Please teach us
to share our bread with those
who do not have any.
Amen.**

For a feast day

† **God our Father,
we are happily gathered here
to celebrate...
We give You thanks for our food
and for the love and joy in our hearts.
Amen.**

When I feel moody

† O Lord Jesus,
  I feel moody tonight.
  There are days when everything
  seems to go wrong,
  and this was such a day!
  So I don't feel like saying
  much to You tonight...
  but I am still Your friend
  and I love You.
  I will try to get to sleep fast
  so I can forget about this day.
  Help me, please,
  make a fresh start tomorrow!
  Amen.

When I am tempted to do wrong

† O Lord Jesus,
  You know me well and You see
  what is going on presently
  in my heart: I feel like doing this...
  even if I know it is wrong.
  I am sure You understand me
  and want to help me.
  Please give me the courage
  to resist that temptation.
  Let Your Spirit rekindle in my heart
  the desire to act right,
  and give me wonderful ideas
  to help others act right too.
  Amen.

When I feel sad

† Lord Jesus,
  I am sad this evening because...
  You, too, were sad sometimes,
  because people did not want
  to listen to You,
  because they tried to hurt You
  and You were not able to make
  Your Dream come true,
  because even Your friends
  let You down during Your Passion.
  Please, Jesus, help me,
  strengthen me.
  I know You are my friend
  and You are always with me;
  I trust in You.
  Amen.

When someone I love is sick

† **Lord Jesus,**
You know... is sick.
Please give him or **her**
courage and patience.
Help the doctors get him or **her**
better quickly.
Show me what I can do
to encourage and comfort...
Amen.

When I am sick

† **Lord Jesus,**
sometimes we feel
like pretending to be sick...
But today I am sick for real,
and truly it's no fun!

Help me be brave enough
not to complain all the time.
Help me be thankful and kind
to those who take care of me.

Lord Jesus,
there are many children
around the world
who are very sick
and have no one
to take care of them;
for them I pray to You
and offer my troubles. Amen.

When someone I love dies

† God our Father,
You created us so we could share
in Your eternal life
and happiness.
Please welcome into Your House...
who has just left this world.
We ask You this
through Christ our Lord. Amen.

† Lord Jesus, You cried
when Your friend Lazarus died.
You understand our grief.
Please help us
in these difficult times, and
teach us how to help one another.
Give special comfort to... and...
who are going to feel very lonely.
Help us all find consolation
in the hope that... is now happy
with You for ever. Amen.

"I am the resurrection and the life.
Whoever believes in Me will live,
even though he dies."　　John 11: 25

To profess my faith

Catholics around the world often express their faith by praying the Apostles' Creed:

† I believe in God, the Father almighty,
   creator of heaven and earth.

I believe in Jesus Christ,
His only Son, our Lord.
He was conceived
by the power of the Holy Spirit
and born of the Virgin Mary.
He suffered under Pontius Pilate,
was crucified, died, and was buried.
He descended to the dead.
On the third day He rose again.
He ascended into heaven, and is seated
at the right hand of the Father.
He will come again to judge
the living and the dead.

I believe in the Holy Spirit, the Holy Catholic Church,
the communion of saints, the forgiveness of sins,
the resurrection of the body, and the life everlasting.
Amen.

You might also like to use this shorter prayer:

† God our Father, Lord Jesus, Holy Spirit,
   You are one in love,
   You save us from evil and death,
   You invite us to share Your own life
   and Your eternal happiness.

We give You thanks and we believe in You.

Praise to the Lord of the Universe

Amidst myriads of stars God gave us for our home the little Planet Earth.
Our Planet Earth is blue, circled with white clouds. It is very beautiful!

Our Planet is a Garden where God would like to see His children live in peace,
happy, free and loving. This is God's own Dream! This is our dream, too!

† **For the sun that gives life
and fills our heart with joy.**
    Praise to You, God almighty!
**For the moon and the stars
which brighten up our nights.**
    Praise to You, God almighty!
**For the song of the wind and the rain
which nourishes the earth.**
    Praise to You, God almighty!
**For the coolness of water
which gives life and refreshes.**
    Praise to You, God almighty!
**For the fish and the birds,
and all living creatures.**
    Praise to You, God almighty!
**For friendship and love, for life and
happiness.**
    Praise to You, God almighty!

Continue the litany as you wish,
then say this closing prayer:

† **God our Father,
You made the universe immense
and beautiful for our happiness.
I give You thanks for its wonders.
I adore You with all my heart,
for no one is like You
in heaven or on earth.
To You praise and glory
for ever and ever! Amen.**

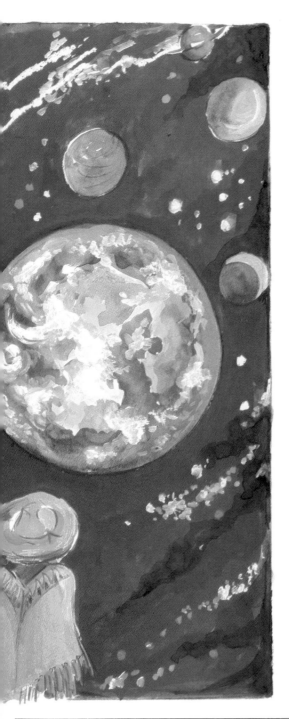

Prayer for our Planet Earth

Unfortunately everything is not right on our planet: every day, on television, we hear about pollution, famine, war, unemployment and crime. There are millions of refugees who have no country, no homes, no bread and no hope. There are people who are too rich and don't share. There are people who are too poor and have nothing. When we see all that is wrong in our world, we should ask God to help us change our hearts and change our world.

† **God our Father,**
  You have entrusted the earth
  to our care,
  and bid us share its riches.
  Give us the courage to make the efforts
  and necessary sacrifices
  to accomplish Your will.
  We ask this
  through Christ our Lord. Amen.

† **Holy Spirit,**
  it is You who changes our hearts,
  and enables us to love.
  Please change the hearts
  of all those who want war,
  who want to take away from others
  their freedom or their bread.
  Strengthen those who suffer
  in their fight against oppression.
  Rekindle in the hearts of all people
  the longing for peace and justice,
  and the courage to build them. Amen.

For the holidays

† Lord Jesus,
holidays are wonderful!
We feel free each morning
to plan our day as we wish.
We can find new friends,
and meet with old ones again.

What do You want of me,
Lord Jesus, during the holidays?
Would it be only that I do my best
to make life enjoyable for all
those around me?
Yes, I believe it is!

Teach me, Lord Jesus,
not to forget anyone,
for parents and other grown ups
also need holidays...
Help me be thoughtful and caring,
so I can make
everyone around me happy.

Lord Jesus,
I thank You with all my heart
for the joy of living,
and the joy of loving.
Amen.